Community Helpers at Work

A Day in the Life of a
Firefighter

by Heather Adamson

Consultant:
Rob Farmer, EMT-P
Firefighter/Paramedic
City of Upper Arlington, Ohio, Fire Division

Capstone
press

Mankato, Minnesota

First Facts is published by Capstone Press,
1710 Roe Crest Drive, North Mankato, Minnesota 56003.
www.capstonepub.com

Books published by Capstone Press are manufactured with paper
containing at least 10 percent post-consumer waste.

Library of Congress Cataloging-in-Publication Data
Adamson, Heather, 1974–
    A day in the life of a firefighter / by Heather Adamson.
    v. cm. —(First facts. Community helpers at work)
    Includes bibliographical references and index.
    Contents: How do firefighters begin their workdays?—What happens when
there is a fire?—Are there ever false alarms?—Where do firefighters eat?—Where do
firefighters sleep?—What do firefighters do when they are not on a fire call?—How do
firefighters put out fires?—What happens after a fire is out?
    ISBN-13: 978-0-7368-2284-8 (hardcover)   ISBN-10: 0-7368-2284-4 (hardcover)
    ISBN-13: 978-0-7368-4673-8 (softcover pbk.)   ISBN-10: 0-7368-4673-5 (softcover pbk.)
    1. Fire extinction—Vocational guidance—Juvenile literature. 2. Fire fighters—Juvenile
literature. [1. Fire fighters. 2. Occupations.] I. Title. II. Series.
TH9148 .A33 2004
628.9'25—dc21   2002155824

Credits
Jennifer Schonborn, designer; Gary Sundermeyer, photographer; Eric Kudalis,
    product planning editor

Photo Credits
Capstone Press / Gary Sundemeyer, cover, 5, 6, 7, 9, 10, 11, 13, 14-15, 16, 19, 20-21
Corbis / Bettmann, 20 (left)
Index Stock Imagery / Carol Werner, cover (background)
Mankato Fire Department, 17

Artistic Effects
Ingram Publishing, PhotoDisc Inc.

Special thanks to firefighter Mark Bergman, the Mankato Fire Department, and the I.A.F.F.
    Local 579 for their cooperation in photographing this book.

Printed in the United States of America in North Mankato, Minnesota.
102011   006437R

Table of Contents

How do firefighters begin their workdays?

Firefighters go to the fire station to start their shifts. Firefighter Mark works from 7:00 in the morning one day until 7:00 in the morning the next day. When Mark arrives at work, he finds his boots and gloves. He checks his air tank to be sure it is full. He must be ready if there is a fire.

Fun Fact:
Famous Americans George Washington, Thomas Jefferson, and Benjamin Franklin all served as volunteer firefighters.

7:00 in the morning

What happens when there is a fire?

10:00 in the morning

People call 911 to report a fire. A dispatcher answers the call and tells the firefighters where to go. The alarm sounds at the station. Mark and the firefighters rush to put on their gear. They drive fire trucks to the fire.

Are there ever false alarms?

Alarms sometimes go off when there is not a fire. Still, people and firefighters must treat every alarm as a real fire. Firefighters check the building to make sure it is safe. Today, Mark's crew spends an hour checking the building. Mark's crew did not find a fire.

Fun Fact:
About 2 million fires are reported in the United States each year.

8

11:30 in the morning

Where do firefighters eat?

12:30 in the afternoon

Firefighters usually eat at the fire station. It is Mark's turn to cook lunch. He makes pasta and bread in the fire station's kitchen.

11

Where do firefighters sleep?

Many fire stations have rooms called dorms where firefighters can sleep. After a short nap, Mark and his crew will train together. They practice rescues and learn how to work safely. Firefighters stay busy even when there are no fires.

2:30 in the
afternoon

5:00 in the evening

ENGINE
COMPANY

What do firefighters do when they are not on a fire call?

Firefighters teach fire safety. Mark shows these children how a fire truck works. He tells them what to do if there is a fire. Firefighters also go to other emergencies. They give first aid and help the police.

How do firefighters put out fires?

 Fun Fact:
Firefighters use special cameras to see through smoke and find trapped people and animals.

Firefighters use special equipment to put out fires. Mark and the driver hook up the hose together. Mark wears a mask and air tank to protect him from smoke. His clothes protect him from heat and spraying water.

17

What happens after a fire is out?

Firefighters have work to do after a fire is out. Mark cleans the trucks. When his shift is over, Mark will go home. Another firefighter will come to work. Firefighters are always on duty.

3:30 in the morning

Amazing But True!

Horses pulled early fire engines. Some fire stations did not have horse stables. If there was a fire, the driver had to run to a nearby field and chase down the horses. After hooking up the horses, the crew raced to the fire.

Equipment Photo Diagram

Ladders

Air Tank

Helmet

Gloves

Boots

Crew Cab
carries firefighters to the fire

Cab
holds the driver and navigator

Hoses

E-905

Dalmatian
Spotted dogs called dalmatians are mascots at some fire stations.

Doors

Glossary

dispatcher (diss-PACH-ur)—a person who answers 911 calls and assigns rescue workers

emergency (e-MUR-juhn-see)—a sudden or dangerous event

equipment (e-KWIP-muhnt)—the machines and tools needed for a job; firefighting equipment includes fire trucks, hoses, and special clothing.

false alarm (FAWLSS uh-LARM)—an alarm that mistakenly sounds when there is no emergency

mask (MASK)—a protective covering worn over the face; some firefighting masks can be hooked to air tanks.

shift (SHIFT)—a set amount of time to work; many firefighters work shifts 24 hours long.

Read More

McGillian, Jamie Kyle. *On the Job with a Firefighter, Neighborhood Guardian*. On the Job with Bridgit & Hugo. Hauppauge, N.Y.: Barron's, 2001.

Wheeler, Jill C. *Firefighters*. Everyday Heroes. Edina, Minn.: Abdo, 2002.

Internet Sites

Do you want to find out more about firefighters and fire safety? Let FactHound, our fact-finding hound dog, do the research for you.

Here's how:
1) Visit *http://www.facthound.com*
2) Type in the **Book ID** number:
   0736822844
3) Click on **FETCH IT**.

FactHound will fetch Internet sites picked by our editors just for you!

Index